D0310941

Don't Forget!

Remembrance Day

Monica Hughes

www.heinemann.co.uk/library
Visit our website to find out more information about **Heinemann Library** books.

To order:
 Phone 44 (0) 1865 888066
 Send a fax to 44 (0) 1865 314091
Visit the Heinemann Bookshop at www.heinemann.co.uk/library to browse our catalogue and order online.

First published in Great Britain by Heinemann Library, Halley Court, Jordan Hill, Oxford OX2 8EJ, a division of Reed Educational and Professional Publishing Ltd. Heinemann is a registered trademark of Reed Educational and Professional Publishing Ltd.

OXFORD MELBOURNE AUCKLAND JOHANNESBURG BLANTYRE
GABORONE IBADAN PORTSMOUTH NH (USA) CHICAGO

Designed by Joanna Sapwell and StoryBooks
Originated by Ambassador Litho Ltd
Printed by Wing King Tong, Hong Kong, China

ISBN 0 431 154023

06 05 04 03 02
10 9 8 7 6 5 4 3 2 1

British Library Cataloguing in Publication Data
Hughes, Monica
      Remembrance Day. – (Don't Forget)
      1. Remembrance Sunday – Juvenile literature
      I.Title
      394 . 2´64

Acknowledgements
The Publishers would like to thank the following for permission to reproduce photographs: Collections/Liba Taylor p. 23; Corbis p. 12; Corbis/Joseph Sohm p. 29; Corbis/Michael St Maur Shiel pp. 10, 11, 15, 17; Corbis/Roger Tidman p. 14; Corbis/Bettmann p. 27; Corbis/Michael John Kielty p. 25; Corbis/Ralph A. Clevenger p. 28; Corbis/Richard Glover p. 13; Garden Matters p. 19; Guelph Museums p. 16; Martin Soukias p. 26, 27; Mirror Pix p. 4; Pa Photos pp. 7, 9; Photofusion p. 5; Photofusion/Bob Watkins p. 18; Pictures of Britain p. 24; Royal British Legion pp. 8, 20, 21, 22; Topham Picturepoint p. 26.

Cover photograph reproduced with permission of Pictor International.

Our thanks to Stuart Copeman for his assistance in the preparation of this book.

Every effort has been made to contact copyright holders of any material reproduced in this book. Any omissions will be rectified in subsequent printings if notice is given to the Publishers.

Contents

Words printed in bold letters, **like this**, are explained in the Glossary.

What is Remembrance Day?

Remembrance Day is on 11 November. It is a special day set aside to remember all those men and women who were killed in the two World Wars and other **conflicts**. At one time the day was known as **Armistice** Day.

Remembrance Sunday is held on the second Sunday in November, which is usually the Sunday nearest 11 November. Special services are held at **war memorials** and churches all over the country. A national ceremony takes place at the Cenotaph in Whitehall, London.

Poppies are sold during October and November

A Remembrance Day march

On both Remembrance Day and Remembrance Sunday people wear red paper poppies pinned to their clothes. There are parades and marches and people lay **wreaths** of poppies at war memorials. The poppies are sold to raise money to help all those injured in war and other conflicts. Look at pages 14 and 15 to find out why we wear poppies to remember the people killed in wars.

Why is it called the Cenotaph?

Cenotaph means 'empty **tomb**'. The word comes from the Greek '*kenos*' meaning empty, and '*taphos*' meaning tomb.

When was the first Remembrance Day?

The First World War lasted for four years between 1914 and 1918. More than 8 million soldiers lost their lives and many more were badly wounded. The **Armistice** was signed in the early hours of 11 November 1918 in a railway carriage standing in eastern France. The battles in the **trenches** were still going on at the time of the signing and so it was agreed that fighting would stop at exactly 11 o'clock. This was the 11th hour of the 11th day of the 11th month.

The first Remembrance Day was held one year later in 1919. It was known as Armistice Day.

First World War soldiers leaving a trench to go into battle

What does it mean?

Armistice means an agreement to stop fighting in a war or battle. It comes from two **Latin** words: '*arma*' meaning weapons and '*sistere*' meaning stop. Other words we use with a similar meaning are truce, cease-fire and peace.

On 11 November 1918, Trafalgar Square in London was packed with **civilians** and **servicemen** on leave. Work stopped for the day. From 1919 to 1945, 11 November became known as Armistice Day. It was renamed Remembrance Day after the Second World War.

Celebrating the end of the First World War in London

What is the two-minute silence?

During the two-minute silence everyone remembers those who have died in **conflicts** or been injured by wars. People have time to pause and be grateful for peace and freedom and to think about others that may not be so fortunate.

The first two-minute silence took place at 11am on 11 November 1919. Sir Percy Fitzpatrick, whose son was killed in France in 1917, suggested it to the government in memory of all those who died in the recent war. The King, George V, asked for 'a complete suspension of all activities' (for everything to stop).

The two-minute silence was **observed** every year from 1919 until it was stopped because of the Second World War (which lasted from 1939 to 1945).

Children observing the two-minute silence

The two-minute silence in a supermarket

After the Second World War things gradually changed and many people observed the two-minute silence on Remembrance Sunday instead of on 11 November. Fifty years after the end of the Second World War a campaign was started to have it **reinstated** at 11am on 11 November.

The first two-minute silence in London, 11 November 1919

'The first stroke of eleven produced a magical effect. Someone took off his hat, and ... the rest of the men bowed their heads also ... An elderly woman, not far away, wiped her eyes, and the man beside her looked white and stern. Everyone stood very still ... The hush deepened. It had spread over the whole city ...'

Manchester Guardian, 12 November 1919.

What is Remembrance Sunday?

Wreaths of poppies on the Cenotaph

On Remembrance Sunday (the second Sunday in November) there are remembrance ceremonies all over the country. There are marches and parades in both large towns and small villages. Local groups take part, often carrying flags and sometimes with bands playing as everyone marches. Ex-**servicemen** and women take part proudly wearing their service uniforms. Most ceremonies end at the local **war memorial** where the different groups lay **wreaths** and poppies.

Medals worn with pride on Remembrance Day

A very large remembrance ceremony is held at the Cenotaph in London on Remembrance Sunday. There is an impressive march-past of servicemen and women. They all wear their uniforms and many also wear medals. The Queen lays a wreath at the Cenotaph and so do many other important people.

A second Remembrance Day

Jewish people hold their Remembrance Day ceremony on the third Sunday in November instead of the second. Jewish men and women of the Army, Air Force and Navy march down Whitehall and place wreaths of poppies at the Cenotaph.

What is the Grave of the Unknown Soldier?

Millions of men were killed during the First World War. Many were buried where battles took place in northern France and Belgium. There are military **cemeteries** in these places now. Over half of those killed were never **identified**. These soldiers were simply buried where they lay on the battlefield.

On the second anniversary of the **Armistice** on 11 November 1920, a special funeral took place to remember all those with no official grave. The remains of an Unknown Soldier were brought back to England and buried in Westminster Abbey in London. Every year **wreaths** of poppies are placed on **tombs** of Unknown Soldiers on Remembrance Day.

Tomb of the Unknown Soldier at Arlington, USA

Gravestones

The words: *'Soldier of the Great War Known Unto God'* were written on the headstone of every First World War grave where the body of the soldier could not be identified.

There are many other tombs to Unknown Soldiers around the world. In France there is one in the Arc de Triomphe in Paris, and in the USA at Arlington Cemetery. On the 75th anniversary of the Armistice an Australian Unknown Soldier was taken from a cemetery in northern France and placed in the Tomb of the Unknown Soldier in the Australian **War Memorial** at Canberra.

The Arc de Triomphe in Paris, France

Why do we have poppies for remembrance?

The First World War was fought in northern France. The soldiers on both sides fought from **trenches** dug into the ground. The battles quickly turned the fields of northern France into a sea of mud in the winter. The land had been so devastated by the fighting that there were no houses, farms, hedges or fields left. Everything was destroyed.

The battlefields of the First World War were very depressing places where nothing grew; nothing, that is, except poppies. Each May when the weather got warmer, red poppies grew in the parched earth. Poppies are one of the few plants that will grow in very poor soil.

Wild poppies growing in fields

Cemetary of soldiers killed at the Battle of the Somme, France

The poppies seemed to comfort those soldiers who were still fighting. Poppies became a **symbol** of hope to the soldiers and a reminder of the many friends who had died in the war. The battlefields were covered with thousands of graves marked by simple wooden crosses. Blooming between them were wild poppies that made the fields a blaze of colour.

Who are the poppies for?

Poppies became a symbol of remembrance of all those who died in First World War. They are now used as a reminder of all those who have lost their lives in war and other **conflicts**. Today the poppy is a symbol of hope for peace and freedom.

15

In Flanders Fields

Captain John McCrae was a professor of medicine and a medical officer with the First Canadian Army who worked in France during the First World War. He was very sad at the deaths of so many young soldiers, particularly after the second battle of Ypres (say 'ee-pr') in Belgium. He tore a page from his **dispatch book** and wrote his famous poem, *In Flanders Fields*.

The poem was about the soldiers who fought and died in Flanders in Belgium. McCrae did not want people to forget what the soldiers had been fighting for. His poem asked people to remember the dead of the First World War, and in the last verse to carry on fighting for their beliefs.

Captain John McCrae

McCrae died in a hospital on the channel coast of France in view of the white cliffs of Dover. He is buried in a **cemetery** in Wimereux, France.

View from the air of how a First World War battlefield looks today

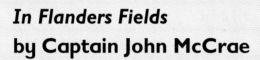

In Flanders Fields
by Captain John McCrae

In Flanders fields the poppies blow
Between the crosses, row on row,
That mark our place: and in the sky
The larks, still bravely singing, fly
Scarce heard amid the guns below.

We are the Dead. Short days ago
We lived, felt dawn, saw sunset glow,
Loved, and were loved, and now we lie
In Flanders fields.

*Take up our quarrel with the **foe**:*
To you from failing hands we throw
The torch: be yours to hold it high.
If ye break faith with us who die,
We shall not sleep, though poppies grow
In Flanders fields.

The first poppies

In 1918, an American called Moina Michael read the poem *In Flanders Fields* by John McCrae, and then wrote her own poem called *The Victory Emblem*. Moina's poem said that red poppies were a **symbol** of the blood of the brave soldiers who died in the war. It called on people to wear a red poppy in honour of those who had died. She wanted to make sure that those who died were not forgotten.

Moina Micheal bought 25 real red poppies and sold these to her friends. They were the first people to wear poppies.

Servicemen and women in a Remembrance Day parade

Madame Guérin was a French secretary at the **YMCA**. She was the first to suggest that **artificial** poppies were made and sold to help needy ex-**servicemen**, women and their **dependants**. Poppies were sold on 11 November 1921 and raised £106,000. The artificial poppies came from France. The money raised from selling the poppies went to help children whose lives had been devastated by war.

In 1922, Major George Howson had the idea of getting five disabled **veterans** to make the artificial poppies. Within a few months there were 50 people making poppies in a factory in Richmond near London.

Poppies

There are more than 100 different kinds of real poppies. They grow wild in fields but are also planted in gardens. Field poppies are always red, but others can be white, yellow, orange, pink or purple.

Poppies today

The poppies used in Remembrance Day celebrations today are all made at the **Royal British Legion** Poppy Factory in Richmond. Poppies are made all year round by the 90 people who work at the factory, many of whom are disabled. Altogether, more than 30 million poppies are made each year.

Making a wreath at the British Legion factory

How money is raised?

Poppies are sold from the middle of October until Remembrance Sunday by the Royal British Legion. The Annual Poppy Appeal raises money that goes to help **servicemen** and women and their families who have suffered as a result of wars or **conflict**.

The poppies have paper petals and paper leaves that are cut by machine. The stem, petals, leaves and button centres are then all put together. Each poppy is made individually by hand. There are several different sizes of poppy, including ones for wearing on your coat, or larger ones for putting in your window or car. **Wreaths** are also made for guides and scouts and other groups. Special wreaths are made for the royal family and other important people.

Enjoying making poppies

What is the Festival of Remembrance?

On the second Saturday in November, a special Festival of Remembrance is held in London at the Royal Albert Hall. It is held in memory of all those who died while serving in both World Wars and other **conflicts**.

Men and women who served in the armed forces during the wars take part, wearing their uniforms. Many of them also wear medals that they have been awarded for bravery and courage. Members of the royal family also attend the festival and they wear black clothes as a sign of respect and **mourning**.

Festival of Remembrance, Royal Albert Hall, London

A Remembrance Day march

There are marching bands playing military music, hymns and prayers and a procession of flags carried by members of the **Royal British Legion**. The Festival of Remembrance is often very moving and ends with hundreds of red poppy petals falling from the ceiling as a reminder of all those who have suffered as a result of war.

The Remembrance Garden

In the week leading up to Remembrance Sunday, a special Remembrance Garden is opened in the grounds of Westminster Abbey. Each branch of the armed forces is allocated a space in the garden. It is then 'planted' with small crosses with poppies on them, in memory of those who died.

23

War memorials

In towns and cities all over the country there are
war memorials. These were erected to remember
those people who died in both World Wars and other
conflicts. The names of the men and women who
died are often found on a war memorial.

There are many different kinds of memorials. Some
are simple straight pillars or columns of stone, like
the Cenotaph in London. Others are more like statues,
sometimes of people in uniform or animals. Many are in
or near the centre of a village, town or city – perhaps in
a public park or garden. In November they become the
places for Remembrance Day services when **wreaths**
of poppies are laid on them.

A village war
memorial

Special gates

There are new memorial gates on Constitution Hill near Buckingham Palace. The gates are a memorial to the men and women of the Indian **sub-continent**, Africa and the Caribbean who fought in both World Wars.

There are also large memorial gates. The Menin Gate in Ypres is engraved with the names of 55 thousand British soldiers who died in the First World War. There are also many simple memorial **plaques** all over Britain and other countries that give the names of the people that have died.

The Menin Gate in Ypres

25

Who do we remember?

On Remembrance Day we remember the great bravery of many men and women.

We remember those who fought and died in the First World War. People like the poet Wilfred Owen who was awarded the **Military Cross**. He was killed a week before the **Armistice** was signed. Or sepoy subahdar Khuda Dad Khan who, although wounded, manned his machine-gun post after all his companions were killed. He was awarded the **Victoria Cross** for his bravery.

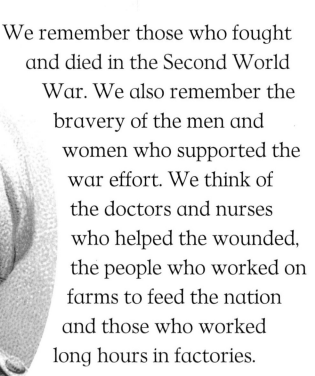

We remember those who fought and died in the Second World War. We also remember the bravery of the men and women who supported the war effort. We think of the doctors and nurses who helped the wounded, the people who worked on farms to feed the nation and those who worked long hours in factories.

Sepoy subahdar Khuda Dad Khan

26

British troops in the Falklands War in 1982

Those who fought in more recent **conflicts** are also remembered. People like Colonel 'H' Jones who was killed in the Falklands War, and Simon Weston who was badly burnt when his ship was bombed in the same war. We also remember all those whose lives have been shattered by war including the many **refugees** who have been made homeless.

From *For the Fallen* (September 1914) by Laurence Binyon

'They shall grow not old as we that are left grow old;
Age shall not weary them nor the years condemn.
At the going down of the sun and in the morning
We will remember them.'

Remembrance Day around the world

Remembrance celebrations take place on 11 November all around the world. Some countries have also set aside another day for remembrance.

In Australia and New Zealand, a public holiday, called ANZAC Day, is celebrated on 25 April. This is a reminder of the day when 11 thousand soldiers from the Australian and New Zealand Army Corps (ANZAC) were killed at Gallipoli in Turkey in the First World War. Armed forces parade in Canberra in front of the National **War Memorial**.

An ANZAC Day parade in Australia

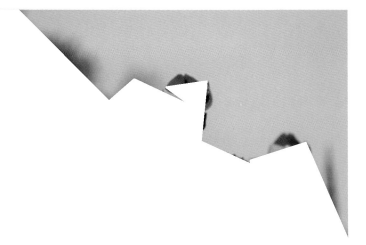

Cub scouts at a Veterans Day gathering in the USA

In America a day is set aside to remember all those who have served their country in war. It used to be called **Armistice** Day but is now known as **Veterans** Day. At one time it was **observed** on the fourth Monday in October but since 1978 it has been celebrated on 11 November.

oldiers from across the world

During both World Wars soldiers came from all over the world to join the British Forces. Many were from the **Commonwealth** and came from as far away as the West Indies and Canada, the Indian **sub-continent**, west, central and southern Africa, Australia and New Zealand.

 Glossary

Armistice   agreement to stop a battle or war

artificial   not real, made by someone

cemeteries (cemetery)   places where bodies
  are buried

civilians   people who are not in the armed forces

Commonwealth   group of countries with special
  links to Britain

conflicts   disagreements, fights or battles

dependants   people who rely on others

dispatch book   official notebook

foe   enemy

identified   recognized who a person is

Latin   language of ancient Rome

Military Cross   medal awarded for bravery

mourning   showing sadness at the death of a person

observed   kept and/or celebrated

plaques   special plates fixed to a wall

refugees   people who are made homeless by war

reinstated   brought back into use

Royal British Legion   organization that helps
  ex-servicemen and women

servicemen   men who serve in the Navy, Airforce
  and Army

sub-continent   part of a continent

symbol   sign with a special meaning

tomb grave, often of someone famous

trenches long narrow ditches dug into the ground

veterans person who has served in the armed forces

Victoria Cross highest medal awarded for bravery

war memorials monuments, statues or plaques put up to remind others of those who have died in war

wreaths rings of flowers or leaves

YMCA Young Men's Christian Association

 # Index

Titles in the *Don't Forget* series:

Hardback   0 431 15401 5

Hardback   0 431 15403 1

Hardback   0 431 15405 8

Hardback   0 431 15400 7

Hardback   0 431 15404 X

Hardback   0 431 15402 3

Find out about other Heinemann titles on our website www.heinemann.co.uk/library

Hyde Valley House